# THE SEVEN DAY PROGRAM TO CHANGE YOUR LIFE

## The Mental Diet

D1736249

# THE SEVEN DAY PROGRAM TO CHANGE YOUR LIFE

## THE MENTAL DIET

BY TONY LEGGETT
WITH ARIANE COMSTOCK

HUMANICS PUBLISHING GROUP
ATLANTA, LAKE WORTH

Humanics Publishing Group

The Mental Diet 7 Day Program to Change Your Life
© 2011 by Tony Leggett with Ariane Comstock
Humanics Publising Group Publication
First Edition

Humanics Publising Group is a division of Brumby Holding, LLC.
Its trademark, consisting of the word "Humanics" and portrayal
of a Pegasus is registered in the U.S. Patent and Trademark
Office and in other countries.

Brumby Holding, Inc.
PO Box 1608
Lake Worth, FL 33460
USA

Website: www.humanicspub.com
email: humanics@mindspring.com


Printed in the United States of American and the United Kingdom

ISBN 978-0-89334-889-2

Photography by Sadu Frehm

THIS BOOK IS DEDICATED
TO MY WONDERFUL READERS,
FROM WHOM I HAVE LEARNED SO MUCH.

# CONTENTS

INTRODUCTION | 1

BEFORE YOU BEGIN | 3

DAY ONE | 9 Activities
14 Explanations
21 Change Your Mind, Change Your Life

DAY TWO | 27 Activities
31 Explanations
37 The Love Stuff

DAY THREE | 41 Activities
44 Explanations
48 The God Connection

DAY FOUR | 53 Activities
57 Explanations
63 You Get What You Think You Deserve

DAY FIVE | 67 Activities
70 Explanations
74 Enough is Never Enough

DAY SIX | 79 Activities
83 Explanations
88 Learning to Listen--to Yourself

DAY SEVEN | 95 Activities
99 Explanations
103 The Up Side of Down

# WHO IS TONY LEGGETT?

For 28 years as "Dear Tony" with the National Examiner, Tony Leggett has been one of America's favorite advice columnists, answering thousands of letters each month with his unique brand of psychic and psychological insight, common sense and compassion. He is a popular guest on radio and TV shows and is an active volunteer for charitable causes.

Readers and audiences alike feel a personal connection to this charismatic media personality who has the ability to translate the wisdom of the ancients into everyday life.

After 50 years as a spiritual healer, Tony still has one ambition: "I just want to help as many people as I can." This book offers you the benefit of all his years of experience.

British born, now an American citizen, and widely traveled, Tony now makes his home in West Palm Beach, Florida.

Tony's personal magnetism, wide experience and his metaphysical research have enabled him to fulfill his dream. Now he enables you to fulfill yours with his inspiring message of hope, love and faith in the future.

# INTRODUCTION

I know what people are looking for: to feel truly alive.

I see inside people and know what they are thinking. After 50 years of being a spiritual healer and over 28 years as a national newspaper advice columnist, I have an excellent idea of what people want – and what people need.

The thousands of people who write to me every week focus on three things: how can they feel better, make money, and how can they change themselves and go from who they are to who they would like to be.

Many people are stuck, victims of the "poor me-isms" from living the down side of life. This brings on sickness and distress, and I hear all about their suffering. Many of these people will stay stuck forever, unhappy with their lives but not knowing how to do anything about it. They are closed off from new ways of thinking, they are feeling lost and helpless.

But then there are some people, like you, who are ready to make the change, who are ready to be shaken free from feelings of doubt and self-pity and ready to learn to look at life, and themselves, in new ways.

I want to help you with this journey. I am passionate about life, passionate about my seven day program, and ready to help you break through the fear that is holding you back. As you will read in this book, I, too, have suffered and have known fear. I, too, thought that there was no way to change my life. But I have found that faith and persistence are the antidote to fear.

If you want something badly enough you can get it with hard work, faith, and a sense of humor. If you really dedicate yourself, like I have, to conquering this fear, you will feel a tingling of new energy, an aura of excitement, a zest for life that you have never experienced before.

I know you can follow my program to a better life. Instead of falling prey to the "why-you-can't", let the "cans" be the driving force. I have seen other people change their lives. I have changed my own. Why don't you go the extra mile with this program and see what you are made of?

I will be with you every step of the way. Remember to put love into everything you do, whether you "like" it or not. We're in for a magic carpet ride!

With much love –
Tony Leggett

# STOP!
## BEFORE YOU BEGIN

Congratulations! You are taking the first step towards truly changing your life just by picking up this book. My seven day program is designed to open up your mind, body and spirit to all the possibilities in life, and help give you the strength to make positive changes. You will actually enjoy the journey of life, instead of just waiting to get to your destination.

If you are depressed, bored, or stuck in a down cycle, you may have already turned to other self-help programs to try to jump-start your life. And they probably didn't work (or you wouldn't be reading this book!). Other programs tell you to spend more money, take time off of work, drastically change your life so that you will find happiness. But you won't find peace of mind that way. Let me instead show you how to break out of your rut and really live life to the fullest - one step at a time,

Everything in this book has been practiced successfully over and over again. My seven day program doesn't cost money. It doesn't take up much time. It doesn't ask you to do anything drastic. You won't crash at the end of the week; in fact you'll even want more! My program is natural, stimulating, and a lot of fun. The secret is in its simplicity - it really works! The only thing you need is *commitment* and *discipline*. You may be tempted to leave out a step, or to do things in a different order. All I ask of you is to approach this week with an open mind, and a commitment to following the program *exactly as it is written here*. If you aren't prepared to do this, then you might as well not even start. Is it too much to ask, though, for a chance to completely turn your life around?

This program is structured in such a way that you will achieve the maximum results in the shortest period of time. And to achieve even greater results, you can do this program again and again. The more times you do it, the more beneficial it will be to you.

It is best to begin this program on a Friday, so you will see that this book is divided up into seven days beginning on a Friday.

Every day begins with a list of activities to do throughout the day, followed by a list of explanations that will tell you why I think it is important to do these activities. I want you to go through the day's activities without reading the explanations until the end of the day. No cheating! Reading the explanations before doing the activities will block the natural flow of events during the day. Read them instead at night, when the day is done and you can reflect on your experiences. I've also included a special chapter to read at any time throughout the day, whenever you have a quite moment, which will help give you inspiration, hope, and strength to continue with this program. Read these words before you fall asleep, first thing in the morning, right when you get to work, whenever you want - they will help put you in a positive, excited mood about the changes you are making in your life.

I will be asking you to do a lot of fun, yet challenging things throughout the day. It is important to embrace these activities enthusiastically and get the most out of them.

I've also included two "Real Thoughts" throughout your day, one in the morning - the A.M. Real Thought - and one in the afternoon - the P.M. Real Thought. These are important points to ponder in depth. The average person has about 7,000 thoughts per day. Some are important, most not. In this exercise, Real Thoughts are profound. They are there to help you realize all that the thought brings up - emotions, buried memories, unexplored feelings, happy times. The realizations stemming from the Real Thoughts plant the foundation for the changes that you will achieve from this program.

I'd like to add a special note about affirmations. You will notice that every day begins and ends with an affirmation. An affirmation is a statement meant to imprint a fact on your mind. It is a declaration of the truth. It may not be the truth as you know it to be at that very moment; however, it is a creative statement of what you desire your circumstances to be, a statement of the way you would like things to be at this very time. I have given you seven affirmations in my program. After you finish the program, you can create your own affirmations to help you in daily life. You can create an affirmation for anything. You can say "I now have a steady job," even if you don't. The more you say it, the sooner you will have this job! And don't forget to do it with love.

An important question often asked is how much time and effort a person should focus on his or her affirmation. It varies for each individual. Time is not really the issue. The key to a successful affirmation is acceptance, acceptance that it is the truth of your being, not just a whim. It could take a day, a week, a month, or an instant. It starts out as a belief and then becomes an inner knowing that is fact. In any case, these are the important things to remember when creating an affirmation:

#1. Know what you want or desire.

#2. Know what you want will not hurt or infringe on the will or well-being of anyone else.

#3. Create a statement or series of statements that declare what you want - in the present tense. It should ultimately be for your    highest good and growth.

#4. Repeat your affirmation until you inwardly know the truth and be thankful for the seed that has been planted.

You are about to embark on a very exciting journey. If you follow this program, friends, family, and co-workers are going to notice a big change in you. They may make fun or criticize. They will say you seem "different", because you will *be* different. You are changing into a better you - so good luck, and enjoy my 7-day program. This is your life – live it, and love it!

**FRIDAY**

# AFFIRMATION: DIVINE ORDER HAS ENTERED INTO MY LIFE. AND SO IT IS.

#1.  Upon rising, wash and dress.

Clean your teeth using your toothbrush with the hand opposite to the one you usually use. Do this every morning through the program - and don't forget!

Smile at yourself and say "I love you!"

#2.  No matter what size and shape you are, eat a well-balanced, tasty, nutritious breakfast. (A cup of coffee and a doughnut is *not* a well-balanced breakfast.) Your body DESERVES the best of food.

#3.  Go for a ten minute walk before you start your normal day.

Take the family along if you must, but it would be better to go alone.

Make a point of noticing what's around you, the world in all its glory.  See the good, not the bad.  Think in the moment – not what was or what is to be.

WALLOW in Mother Nature's gifts.

**A.M. Real Thought (at morning break):** *Think of all the good things that are in your life.*  Keep a diary handy, and make a written list of them, and from time to time during this week, add to it as things come to mind.

#4.  At lunchtime, get yourself something different to eat. Open up your mind to something really different that could  tantalize your taste buds and make you feel good. Don't tell yourself that you can't afford it; you don't have to spend a lot of money - just try something new.

Eat slowly and and chew each mouthful 40 times. Think happy thoughts of someone you love - or would like to love.

**P.M. Real Thought (at afternoon break):** *When was the last time I had a really good laugh?* On a scale of 1 to 10, how do you rate your sense of humor? Think back to how your sense of humor used to be - was it better or worse than it rates now? Why? Write your answers in your diary.

#5. For the rest of the day, *smile*.

Smile everywhere you go and at everyone whom you meet. You might even add a "Hi" to strangers.

Whether you are collecting your pay or in the supermarket spending money, out to dinner - keep on smiling. Others may think that you have gone slightly crazy, and you may have sore cheek muscles, but don't worry about them - remember, you are working on *you* this week.

When you eventually go to bed make sure that smile is on your face when you fall sleep. Clear your mind, and SMILE. You will sleep with the angels.

Rejoice in the feeling!

#6. It's Friday, and you will be thinking about the weekend.

It's going to be a weekend of "play". Whether you have housework or shopping to do, a ballgame to go to, or you are just staying at home - whatever you are doing, PLAY!

Have some fun, dress up, change your appearance, fantasize. And make some of the happier fantasies come true.

You may have trouble warming up your family and friends to your wacky weekend, but don't let them put you off. When it comes down to it, there is only one person who can make you happy - and that is *you*. If you are expecting happiness to come from someone else, you could wait forever.

Play, be silly - HAVE FUN! And *smile*.

#7. On your way home, buy some flowers or a little present for yourself. Yes, for YOU! It's time you learned to receive, and not feel guilty about it.

Enjoy your gift. Appreciate it.

#8. Make sure you have this evening free so you can do what you want. Go with the flow; but don't sit home waiting for others to make things happen – start the ball rolling yourself.

Do something to yourself that makes your appearance different - different clothes, or a different hairstyle. Be a new person this Friday night; keep that in mind all evening. Remember that if you are bored, then it is you who are boring. Life is like the movies - produce your own show.

*And make it a good one!*

#9. When you go to bed, put that smile on your face and wear something sexy and soft, even if it's just body lotion, so that you feel sexy and soft – male or female.

And remember, just before you go to sleep say "Thank you, God" (or whomever you believe in). And also say "thank you" to yourself for allowing yourself to make this move for the better.

And know that it is already happening. You are opening up to the Universal Good.

**Repeat affirmation:** *Divine order has entered my life.*

# Explanation for Day One
*(to be read after completing the program)*

#1. "Clean your teeth using your toothbrush with the hand opposite to the one you usually use".

Athletic coaches advise athletes that if they are losing, they need to shake up their life and their attitude by making some kind of change, whether it is wearing a different pair of shoes or socks or doing what tennis champion Chris Evert did - she once said that she had a "melody in her head" when she was battling for a championship. If she was losing, she switched songs.

A thing as simple as changing the hand with which you brush your teeth can make you think about what you are doing, and change your attitude toward the whole day. It is an adventure!

Those smiles not only exercise your face muscles; they attract smiles from others as well.

#2. "Eat a well-balanced, tasty, nutritious breakfast."

You are what you eat. If, on this one day, you eat what your body needs instead of what you think you want, you are bound to feel good about it. And that feeling will carry over into the rest of day, if you let it. How did you feel today after you ate a good breakfast? Keep in mind that your body is different from any other body, and remember to fuel it with the life force that makes you work best.

#3. "Go for a ten-minute walk…"

We all know that exercise is good for us, but few people really want to do it, or even enjoy it. New discoveries indicate that just ten minutes of activity can improve your health and sense of well-being, and can even extend your life. Walking is important because, not only do you get the benefits of exercise, but you get to notice your surroundings in a whole new way. As you walk, you breathe deeply, your blood pulsates through your body, and you absorb the ambiance of your environment - this helps you focus your attention and visualize your greater potential. When you are uptight or upset, your body "closes down" and will not work naturally. Walking just ten minutes a day will help you relax - exercise frees your body and your mind. Plus, it's a "feel good" move.

**A.M. Real Thought:** *"Think of all the good things that are in your life."* Counting our blessings is the first step toward a positive attitude. You will be amazed at how many things you will find to be thankful for. This gratitude is a "magic quality" that will give you inner strength and security.

Most people have more good happen to them on a daily basis than bad. But most of the people who talk to me are blind to this fact. Seeing and recognizing the good in your life will attract even more good to you. It's a natural law, and one of life's best-kept secrets.

#4. *"Get yourself something different to eat."*

Opening the mind to the senses is a way of embracing life - and allowing it to embrace you in return. Really tasting your food is also the first step toward controlling your diet and making you feel better about yourself. Allow yourself to enjoy your food; after all, it is nourishing the temple in which you live. Lavish as much care and attention on that temple as you would on your own home. Not only eating the proper foods, but the way in which they are consumed makes the body's digestion work better and generates an over-all positive feeling. This leads to a happier, healthier life – and a trimmer body.

**P.M. Real Thought:** "…Rate your sense of humor…"

Laughter is the best medicine; very rarely do you find

anyone who laughs a lot becoming sick for very long. Too many people have lost the habit of laughter. Laughter is infectious; it creates camaraderie, it is good exercise and it sends out endorphins to every part of the body that will make you feel good.

#5. "For the rest of the day, smile."

Did you know that a smile takes only 14 muscles, while a frown needs 72! If you are lazy or worried, that alone is reason enough to smile. But more important, a smile is a natural face lift - it lifts the facial muscles, counter-acting gravity, while a frown drags your muscles, and everyone around you, down. Try smiling in the mirror. Most people don't like the way they look. Try on a smile, and see how much better you look! Others will see you that way, too, and you will get a positive response..

Many psychiatrists claim that your expression can actually cause you to feel an emotion. Frowning makes you feel cross and sad. Smiling will make you feel happy. And it will make others happy, too. A smile is like a welcome mat at the door - it invites others to share in your happiness, and welcomes joy, love and peace into your life and the lives of all those who benefit from your happy smile. Smiling is the first step towards attracting these positive forces. How did you feel today when you smiled? Did others notice your happiness and return your smile with one of their own? I'll bet they did.

#6. "…A week-end of play."

Who said that life had to be serious? Were you excited today thinking that you are setting aside the weekend as a time to play and have fun? Did it help make your work today more enjoyable? It is important to maintain this attitude of joyfulness and fun, whether you are at work or at home on the weekends. Try to recapture that excitement you felt as a child when you used to play at being "grown up." Other people may not understand your free-spirited, fun-loving attitude, but don't let them get you down. Maybe they will come around and laugh at life with you! It's a healing force. The difference in you will make a difference in them.

#7. "Buy a little present for yourself."

Did buying yourself a present today make you happy? It should, because you deserve it! Feeling good about yourself builds self esteem, and self esteem gets the good stuff flowing, and attracts more of the same.

#8. "Be a new person…"

With this in mind, stop spending your whole life trying to make others happy. Concentrate more on what makes <u>you</u> happy. Those around you tend to be happy if you are. This week is your special time; be different - let your family and friends think about you. If their comments this week are, "What's going on? You seem different," then these are the outward signs that the good changes are already taking place.

#9. "…wear something sexy and soft…"

Feeling sexy and soft in bed is important, even if you sleep alone. It means that you are open to enjoying the real physical nature God gave you, in the security of your own bed. You will then be able to relax peacefully into the natural healing of sleep. Man or woman, feeling comfortable and happy in bed should be natural. Going to bed feeling angry or ugly will only enhance those negative feelings. Going to bed happy will attract sleep, and bring about a feeling of well-being. You spend a third of your life in bed, and that is one-third that you can control. So make it a happy experience.

And don't forget, tomorrow starts another new day! Inspire yourself to be the best you can be, whatever you do - I'll help, if you let me.

# CHANGE YOUR MIND, CHANGE YOUR LIFE

I want to tell you a story about how my life was radically altered when I realized the most important lesson I will ever learn: that life is never static, never the same, but a continuing stream of changes and new experiences. It is how well we accept and even embrace these changes and challenges that will determine whether we have a full, fruitful, successful life, or one filled with terror of the unknown.

Around thirty years ago, my good life as it was then (traveling the world, rubbing elbows with the rich and famous) collapsed. I was on the verge of suicide because I could see no way out of my misery. The change in my life was so vast that it produced a paralyzing fear that threw everything into darkness.

I did everything wrong; I stuck my head in the sand, panicked, felt like a victim, didn't listen to anyone who would tell me that I should live life one day at a time, that I would get through this troubled time. I thought that death was my only way out.

I relocated and tried to find a new career, all the while still scared of the changes in my life. At this time, I joined a Toastmasters group, an organization that teaches you how to speak in public.  This was an ironic decision, for it is a fact that the second greatest fear people have, after death, is of speaking in public.  Here I was, staring death in the face as I thought about suicide, and also choosing to try my hand at public speaking.  I was scared of both - death and speaking in public - but the second fear turned out to be my saving grace, and helped wipe out my first fear.  Within eight weeks of joining Toastmasters, I was in the Florida State Finals.  I found out that, despite my fears, not only could I speak in public, but that I was really good at it.  Now, years later, no one can shut me up!

There are several things I could have done.  I could have remained terrified of the changes in my life and never left the house, wallowing in my pain and convinced that it was bad Karma.  I could have refused to join Toastmasters because I was scared of public speaking.  I could have joined, but not tried my hardest to do well.  I could even have taken the extreme route of suicide.  But I chose instead to be the master of my own ship - my life - and ride the waves, taking on the challenges at this time even when my confidence was crushed and my sense of humor was battered.  I took a chance on myself, took a chance that I could turn the negative changes into something positive.  And guess what - I was able to create a new life for myself, set myself down a different and better path. For the first time in my forty years, I felt really alive, because I realized that it was *my choice* in how I dealt with the problems life threw at me.  One step at a time, one day at a time, life really did begin at forty.

I want to be a catalyst for change in your life.  The first forty years of my life - the School of Hard Knocks - taught me a lot about how to deal with change, and opened the doors to the best that life has to offer.  You, too, will see as you get older that experience is the best way to learn which choices to make.  But I can help guide you in the right direction, help you to put aside your fear of change, help you  to roll up your sleeves and get to work creating a more positive attitude that will lead to a richer, more spiritual life in this new Age of Aquarius.

Having gone through it, I know how difficult and frightening change can be.  I also know how important it is to get over this fear, because the fear of change contributes to some of the worst evils in society.  Abused wives stay with their husbands because they are afraid of change.  People stay in boring, depressing jobs because they are scared of looking for new work.  They repeat patterns of alcoholism and drug use, eating disorders and illnesses, because they can't imagine changing these patterns and trying a different way of living.  Or they just sit on the sofa - inertia - because it is simply easier to stay there than to get up and look for different things to do and create a better  life.

Too many people are stuck in a pattern of life that they are afraid to give up, because this pattern is familiar.

They prefer the misery of boredom and unhappiness to the excitement of living life to its fullest, because boredom and unhappiness is all they have ever known. Many people *say* they want to be happy, but their actions prove otherwise. How many people do you know who actually *look* for reasons to be unhappy? It's as if they want to sabotage their chances of having an enriching life, because with all the good changes, there also will be a few painful ones. It is so easy to adopt an attitude of "if it's not broke, don't fix it", instead of looking hard at your life and realizing that there's so much potential there. It is so easy to read the papers and watch the news and live vicariously through the media, and not try to "unstick" yourself from the mire of habit and not only embrace, but seek out change.

But I am here to change all of that. I am here to shout down all the years of negativity that have poisoned us. Most of us are fed on this diet of negativity for the first 18 years of our lives. All we hear is "Don't...", "No, no!" and "You can't." We have to exchange that inner tape in our brains from our well-meaning parents and teachers with a recording that says "Do!" and "Yes!" and "I can!" and "This feels great!" It is all a matter of attitude and of inner preparation.

You aren't going to be able to live life to its fullest until you get your head in order and learn to believe in yourself and your ability to cope with challenge. It's the foundation for contented living. You must be willing to change. You must be excited about the prospect of change.

And you must prepare yourself for the fact that sometimes life throws changes at you that you don't even want. We are all familiar with this kind of change and loss - loss of loved ones, loss of a job, loss of good health. Some of us have been victims of crime and natural disaster. These are forces over which we have little control, forces that can destroy our confidence if we aren't prepared for them.

After reading this book and following my seven day program, you are going to notice a profound difference in your life. You are going to be able to trust in your ability to accept the changes that are happening to you, that they will take you to your fullest potential and highest good. Even if some of these changes hurt, they will ultimately connect you to your spiritual self and make clear your soul's purpose in life. You will approach life like a child does, finding joy in new experiences. A child has no fear of the unknown, only a desire to go there. You can go there too.

When we are stuck, sometimes we need a little shove. Joining Toastmasters was my shove. Let this book be your shove. It's like learning to walk; you start with one baby step at a time, and before you know it, you are running free.

It's really that simple.

**DAY**

# 2

**SATURDAY**

# Affirmation:
# I am safe, happy and loved.

#1. Get out of bed by 8:00 a.m. Make the bed. Do you what you have to do, then take somebody else's dog for a walk.

#2. All day today, you will pretend that you are someone else. It can be anyone – Tom Cruise, Oprah, Jennifer Lopez, Jackie Chan, James Bond - or someone who isn't famous, or someone you invent. Just remember there is one Golden Rule: once you have decided, you have to keep on being that person, no matter what. Think like that person, talk like that person, act like that person. If you slip back to being you, start all over again. Live your fantasy.

#3. Drink the first of your three to six glasses of pure, fresh water for the day. You should get into the habit of drinking this amount every day.

#4. Treat everybody this day as you would like to be treated yourself.

#5. No matter what you have to do in the way of routine, give it a twist in some way, shape or form. See the positive possibilities in each instant.

**A.M. Real Thought:** *Am I eating right?*

#6. Some time this day, do something nice for somebody who really needs it - a shut-in, or somebody who can't do for themselves - and enjoy doing it! Don't see it as a chore, or that you are doing someone a favor. Enjoy it, have fun - remember, you're being a different you.

#7. Today, forgive two people against whom you may have some grudge, no matter how far back you have to go. No ifs, no buts – forgive totally.

#8. Sometime during the afternoon, write down twenty times: "I am safe, happy and loved." It will be wonderful if you write that down every day twenty times for the next six days. After writing it, sit quietly by yourself and listen to the feedback that comes to you. This will make it clearer where you are coming from.

#9. Forgive yourself for something that you did that made you angry and upset this past week.

**P.M. Real Thought:** *I am a good person, and I care.*

#10. This very moment, for no reason, go hug someone!

#11. For this Saturday evening, cook yourself an exotic meal from a foreign country (take-out is acceptable!). Have friends and family join you. If you wish, pretend that you are actually in that country. To add flavor to the mood, dress up and decorate. Don't let anybody say anything bad about anyone else for the rest of the evening.

#12. The rest of the night is yours to do as you see fit. Only remember, play and be happy.

**Repeat affirmation: I am safe, happy and loved.**

# EXPLANATION FOR DAY TWO

#1. To take somebody else's dog for walk is both a fun and trying experience.  First you have to find the dog.  When you do, you will go through the frustration of trying to get this dog to do what you want and go where you want to go.  Try to see this as a fun learning experience instead of a frustrating one.  Make sure that the dog you take is one that you have never walked before.  Your feelings about this experience may reveal a great deal about yourself.

#2. Your great adventure of the day was pretending you were someone else.  Whom did you pick - someone famous and glamorous, your next door neighbor, a family member - or did you invent a person?  Dressing like that person, acting like that person, and most important, thinking like that person, will give you a new perspective on yourself.  Looking at life through their eyes will make you see your own life in a totally different way.  How would they feel about *you* as a person - what would they change about you?

Note how the people around you reacted to your new character. Did they treat you better or worse? Did you care? Don't worry about these people - this is not their drama.  It is *your* empowerment.

Remember how you walked as this character, how you

held your head and reacted - what were your facial expressions? How did it feel to be proud or humble, joyful or tragic, beautiful or brilliant or powerful? How did you, as the character, react to all the things that happened to you today? Would these things have happened to you if you were "playing" yourself?

This exercise is fun, but it is also one of the most meaningful things you can do in your program to change your life. It is almost impossible to view your life clearly from the "inside." You will get a much brighter picture through some one else's eyes.

#3. Water is the most important element of life. Are you in the habit of flavoring your water with sugar, caffeine, or Scotch? Do you only drink it to wash down your meals?

Try savoring it. Drink pure, fresh water as a symbol of the purity of the life force. Drink water as if it gives you life - because it does. Think of the waterfalls, the rushing streams created by melting snow, of the gentle, nourishing rain that gives life to the earth. It cleanses your system as it quenches your thirst.

#4. Of course, you've recognized the Golden Rule here - treating everybody today as you would like yourself to be treated. We have been focusing today on paybacks. The Golden Rule doesn't always work immediately. Remember that pay-backs often come from unexpected sources - and at unexpected times. So be ready and be grateful.

#5. Everyone gets sick of the same old routine. Doing things in a slightly different way may make you remember the original reason why you started your routine in the first place - that it was pleasant, easy, or convenient! From now on, you will have to make a decision - do you want to do things the old way and appreciate your routines, or do you want to try a new way? Just don't be afraid to take chances.

**A.M. Real Thought:** "Eating right" is not necessarily eating the way the latest health fad dictates. Your body knows what you need. The trick is listening to it, and understanding the difference between what your emotions want and what your body needs. It's O.K. to have one chocolate or one drink - pleasure in moderation. But more than that - gorging - is an emotional need, not a physical one. Scientific studies have shown that even children, if left to themselves, will eventually eat correctly - including eating spinach. And so will you.

#6. Have you ever done something nice for someone who didn't appreciate it - held the door for a grumpy old lady, or let someone in ahead of you in traffic who didn't wave thanks? You probably felt cross with them, but good about yourself. You were big enough to grant favors. This exercise will make you realize that you are a big person, one who can afford to give without demanding anything in return. That's your true spiritual self.

#7. Were you *really* able to think back and find a person or persons against whom you carry a grudge, and were you *really* able to forgive? Very often, we treasure our grudges, just as we treasure our misery. It is a strong feeling, and we'd rather feel it than nothing at all. Once you face up to that, you are ready to give up all your pains and aches and grudges, and fill up the void they leave behind with joy, peace and happiness.

#8. Why does everyone find it so hard to forgive themselves? We forgive others on a daily basis. And yet, the least fault in ourselves we find unforgivable. Learn to say, "O.K., I made a mistake." Slap your hand and then forgive - but don't forget, or you'll do it again. The more you learn, the more you'll grow.

**P.M. Real Thought:** It is very important to your subconscious to define the kind of person you are: *a good person*. You wouldn't be reading this book if you weren't a good person - bad people don't worry about getting better! You also care about others.

If you put up a protective shield around yourself and convince yourself that you don't care (because caring can be very painful), then you will be blind to the basic reality of truth, goodness and light in this world.

#9. Hugs are important. I'm not talking about sexual hugs here, but about physical demonstrations of pure affection. This kind of love is essential to all creatures. Even plants grow better when they are loved - and so will you.

You not only need to *be* loved, but you need to express your love for others. If you have no love to give, then you are poor indeed – or at least short-changing yourself. But most of us are rich in our capacity to love - so let's give it freely. A hug costs you nothing, and yet it vastly enriches the huggee.

#10. This was your play-acting day, and you completed it by having a foreign experience. This experience will have enriched your life and the lives of those who participated with you. You will realize that there's a whole world out there, a world for you to reach out to and enjoy. You may be inspired to study the customs, the language, and the people of another part of the world. This too, will enrich your life. See the world with all your imagination and all your heart.

#11. Most of us take life too seriously. Think about it - if you give someone a gift, don't you want them to enjoy it? How would you feel if they put the gift in the closet and never used it, or if they frowned when you gave it to them? God has given you the magnificent gift of life; don't lock it in a closet. He wants you to use it, and enjoy it!

# THE LOVE STUFF

Some years ago, I went to comfort a woman who was dying of cancer. I told her my belief that cancer comes from a long-time hurt or resentment. Some people would rather die from cancer than forgive the person or persons who wronged them so terribly. After a long talk, this woman said, "That's right. I would rather die. I am never going to forgive my husband."

Her husband had been a very famous actor, and he had been unfaithful to her many times. I tried to tell her that her feelings of anger were justified, but was it worth harboring this hate and resentment, which ultimately turned into a horrible sickness? I spoke to her of love and of letting go, and how important it is to feel and express this love before passing away. It is impossible to move on in peace and harmony when you are mired in self-loathing and anger at others. But this woman denied herself a peaceful ending because of her ego - she thought she was punishing her husband by refusing to forgive him, when in fact she was punishing herself. She needed to let go of these hateful feelings and embrace love. Instead, she died in pain, eaten up by an old hurt.

This book will help you understand the deep power of love, and the profound importance it plays in our life. There is so much love that already exists in this world, but unfortunately people let petty angers and jealousies get in the way of their truly experiencing the power of love. They don't know how to tap into the love that exists in themselves and how to share this love with others. People also don't understand that before you can love others in a positive, healing and unconditional way, you first have to first look inward and learn how to nourish love for yourself.

I was asked to visit an elderly woman who was sick and fading fast. The doctors had given up on her and said there was nothing more they could do, which meant in their language that they didn't know what to do next. She had heart problems, and had very little time left.

She was a woman of means, and had been very powerful in her day. When I first met her, though, I could see that while she was wealthy in riches, she was not wealthy in love for herself. She had family and friends who loved her, but she didn't love herself. When I told her that if she wanted to live, she would have to love herself, she said, "That's not proper. I was brought up that that's not the thing to do."

After many meetings and discussions, she became interested in my beliefs, and I explained to her that heart problems come about when you don't love yourself enough. It took some guidance and care, but once she began to like the idea of loving herself, she began to get well, and lived for many more joyful years. When it was time for her to pass on, she died in peace, with love in her heart and a smile on her face. She accepted my challenge to change, and she won in the end.

This woman learned a very important lesson. If you have love for yourself - and it is not being conceited to truly love one's self - you are filled with a mystical power. Love and self-confidence keep anger, fear and depression at bay. Love is fed with faith, hope and kindness. The effort of loving yourself and embracing this goodness spiritually reflects all else that is good in this world. When you sincerely love and feel good about yourself, you will radiate this positive energy. Others will find this aura irresistible, and you will find a soulmate, the right person, who not only responds to your energy but who also has the flow of self-love in himself or herself, too.

Insecure people seek to make love "conquests" out of ego. They don't seek to love, only to be loved, because such conquests boost their sense of self-worth. Once the object is "conquered", they lose interest - because they think anyone stupid enough to love them isn't worth having. These are the people who have trouble loving, because they don't love themselves. They don't understand that the only way you can find happiness is to love someone unconditionally, without demanding anything in return, and to love yourself unconditionally, too. It is the most wonderful feeling.

Many people do not realize that love exists in the forefront of our lives, that it can always be there and does not have to be tied to our relationship with another person. Some expect love to come from other sources. When that person goes away, then all love disappears as well. That is why people suffer so painfully from a broken heart when someone they care for leaves them. If you start with a strong heart and a powerful sense of self-love, though, than the magic of love will not disappear from your life, even if your beloved does. Recognize and admit the hurt, learn from your past experiences, and do not beat yourself up. Don't turn off the flow of love you feel for yourself and for other people. You will find comfort in this love, and will be able to forgive any person who has wronged you with an open heart.

It is vital to nourish this love in yourself and in others. It is an all-consuming and rewarding task. Children should be brought up in this aura of love. Show them how much you care! When I was a child, there was little love expressed in our family. We just didn't know how to do it. My mother and father were brought up with a lack of love and understanding, and so were my sister and I. We were fed and kept clean and warm. But there was little affection, no hugging or kissing. It took me a long time to understand the warmth of love. As I got older and found out about sex, I thought that that was love. I was wrong. After years of fumbles and mistakes and hurt feelings and many other lessons, I began to finally see what love is.

But it doesn't have to be that difficult. Love is fun. Love is life. Love is healing. Loving yourself and others will help you look younger, be happier, feel healthier. Keep the light of love around. Give some of it away to others, and you will be doubly blessed.

**DAY**
**3**

**SUNDAY**

# Affirmation: All is well in my life.

#1. If you can sleep until 8:00 a.m., do so, then get up and eat a good breakfast. Now look around the house for something to throw away, something you don't need anymore. Either give it to someone or throw it in the garbage today.

#2. This Sunday morning, go to a place of worship. If you don't already have your own place of worship, pick any one. If you go to a church on a regular basis, go to some other church. Observe, and don't judge.

#3. On the way home from church, stop and look around you. If there are any animals to feed, get some food and feed them.

**A.M. Real Thought:** *I am close to God, I am loved.*

#4. Sunday afternoon, visit someone that you haven't seen for a long time, someone whom you like. Or write a letter to someone far away.

#5. Amuse yourself today with one or all of these three types of activities:

Some type of action game where you physically participate:

A mental game: Sudoku, chess, or cards.

Something artistic: paint a picture, write some poetry, create a private dance.

#6. Late in the afternoon, rest - put your feet up for awhile, no matter where you are, and reflect on the day.

#7. Sit and listen - really listen - to some light classical music - and make sure it *is* classical - to raise your vibrations and relax in peace.

**P.M. Real Thought:** *Tomorrow starts the new work week, and it's going to be a good one. No matter what goes wrong, I will take it in stride.*

#8. Make a list of the three of the things you have been putting off doing. Sometime during the next five days, do them.

#9. Spend time this evening with someone whom you see as your best friend. Get out all of your old photographs and go back into the past for awhile. Enjoy yourself and feel free – but make sure you're in bed by ten o'clock.

**Repeat affirmation: All is well in my life.**

# EXPLANATION FOR DAY THREE

#1. It is important to rid yourself of "excess baggage", of unnecessary clutter - of garbage, if you will, in your physical life. You know that the spiritual world affects the physical world, but sometimes an action in the physical world has spiritual connotations. The act of "cleaning house" is a symbol that you are preparing for new future. Getting rid of something you've been keeping "just because I might need it some day" is a positive statement of faith. What you need in the future will be provided; it always is.

#2. Sunday is the day of rest that we all need - a clean, shining, different day of relaxation and love. Every human being needs spiritual light. With it, we grow. Without it, the soul withers and dies. Be it one hour on Sunday morning or on a regular daily basis, we all need the God stuff. Love and compassion are the universal message of every religion. So it is good to spend part of this day of your Week of Change in a place where people gather to share in worshipping a higher power. You will gain even more by observing people of *different* faiths on this Sunday. Learn from them, and appreciate them.

#3. Feeling close to nature is just as important as feeling close to God. Did you take time today to smell the flowers, admire the birds and the bees and even the bugs? Remember when you were a small child and there was a whole world in a plot of ground? There still is!

**A.M. Real Thought:** Every being on earth is close to God - and there is no better place to be. When you feel the most alone, that is when He is the closest. All you have to do is call. Repeat this thought until you feel His caring presence.

#4. Distance and time can often separate us from those whose closeness was once meaningful in our lives. Did it feel good to talk to or write to someone special in your life whom you hadn't seen in a long time? Sometimes that little touch that you remember - a phone call, a card - can be important in ways you may not understand. Even if your attempt today was unsuccessful and you didn't get in touch with your old friend or relative, you will be glad you made the effort. And something will come from that.

#5. Teachers always try to stimulate the minds and imaginations of their students. Why should you not do this for yourself? You wouldn't let your car rust away for lack of use - why would you let your imagination deteriorate? Children's games are good for adults too - even better, because you play them better now!

#6. If the Lord could rest on Sunday, you can too. Quiet moments are often hard to come by, but they are necessary if you are going to survive the busy days ahead. Clear the decks for action by erasing all problems in your mind.

#7. Classical music is the best for raising your vibrations. Even vegetables grow better to the melodies of Mozart! There are many kinds of classical music, so experiment until you find the kind that best enhances your own personal inner vibrations and helps you connect with peace.

**P.M. Real Thought:** Positive expectations bring positive results. You have surmounted all the obstacles in your path so far, and you will continue to do so. Don't count the obstacles; count the jumps you have made over them!

#8. Unfinished business is the cobweb in the closet of your mind. You can't see what you have until you get rid of the cobweb. Nothing feels as good as having accomplished something that has been hanging over your head for a long time. Swoosh! It's gone, and you can forge ahead with a clean slate. Don't dwell on "what was".

#9. Hash over the "good old days" with a friend, and you will be amazed at how many great times you've had. This evening, only talk about the good things that have happened and forget about hard times. Concentrate on the happiness that you have enjoyed in the past and leave "poor me" behind. Say "thanks" for the good times, and know that there will be more in the future. And rejoice in the variety of your experiences. You are starting to glow!

# THE GOD CONNECTION

All human beings need spiritual light. With it, they grow. Without it, the soul withers and dies. Be it one hour on a Sunday morning or on a regular daily basis, we all need the God connection.

As a child, my parents gave me the option of either attending church or going to Sunday School. I picked church, because in Sunday School I would have had to read the Bible out loud. I had nothing against the Bible, but I was a poor reader and hated reading in public. When my family decided that Sunday School was best for me, I got angry and fearful, and resented God for putting me in such a rotten situation. I got off on a bad foot with God and organized religion.

I had a change of heart years later while living in Majorca, Spain. I had the "Good Life" there, and yet I always felt that something was missing. I couldn't shake the empty feeling in my life. One beautiful day, I was in a speedboat with two women and a good bottle of champagne. I looked at the blue sky and said, "God, why are you making me so unhappy?" At that moment, I had a great realization. God had given me this wonderful life. It was *me* who was unhappy with *me*. Happiness isn't found in material things, in champagne and women and fast boats and tons of money. These things weren't going to give me peace - only the spirit could give me peace. I felt God's love beyond my wildest dream, and this set me on the right track. After always thinking that marriage was a dead end, I finally got married at the age of 50 to a wonderful woman. The time was right, my partner was right, and I loved being married.

All God's work falls into place when the time is right. It's people who get in the way.

Now that I know the truth, I want to pass that feeling on to all those who feel as empty as I once did. But you first have to be open to the fact that God exists, that there *is* a higher spiritual power. Everybody has been taught about God, but you need to experience God through your heart and intuition and not just through your head and what you read in books. There is proof that a higher power does exist. I know this for a fact because of all the miracles I have seen and experienced through the work I do. Open your mind and heart to this!

I never understand why people are so willing to accept *bad* news - that we have no souls, that there is no afterlife, that the devil exists - and so reluctant to believe *good* news, such as that our spirits never die, and that a higher power exists to give us strength and guide us through life. Some people even scoff at spiritual things. They put faith in science alone, but what is science, except our attempt to discover how nature works? Scientists examine nature, they don't invent nature, and they do so with a closed mind. They would never dream of claiming that a computer "just happened" or that it "invented itself", yet that is what scientists claim about the planet.

They don't see the magical, spiritual force behind the creation of the earth, the miracle that our planet is - even the most brilliant scientists can't imitate how the earth cleans and recycles itself, when humans leave it alone.

All the combined knowledge of mankind since the beginning of time cannot invent, define, or defeat the human spirit. Albert Einstein, one of the most intelligent scientists ever to have lived, understood this, and if God is good enough for Albert Einstein, he is good enough for me too.

While it is important to understand that a God exists, it is also important to understand that God is good and only inspires good things. It is people who bring out the bad, and who misuse the power of God.

A friend once told me her sister-in-law was in the hospital and on the verge of dying. A few well-intentioned friends, all with different religious beliefs, came to do what they could for her. Each person insisted that his or her religious way was the right one, and wasted time in argument. The healing of the sick patient came second to this debate over who was closer to God. All these would-be healers had forgotten what the true source of their inspiration was, and how they could use this to help their friend. If they had prayed together in a circle like my Healing Team, united in God and with no religious ax to grind, then their friend would have benefited sooner from the power of their combined beliefs. God's energies are there for everyone. We just need to shed the trappings of our petty concerns to get to this energy.

Prayer, meditation, and trance states can help you tap into this energy, whether you are alone or with a group. Imagine all the power at your disposal! Did you know that more cures take place through prayer groups than any other single form of healing? That's why I lead my Heal-a-thon each year. Also, when people gather together to pray, traces of the spiritual power that they have invoked remain in that place. Mystical and natural forces are available to you, whether you are in a church, a temple, a mosque or in a power center of nature - on top of a mountain, by the sea - where the raw, dramatic force of nature contributes to the great spiritual energy in our lives.

Calling upon these forces in prayer can bring about powerful healings, but be sure to word your prayers thoughtfully and with love.

Remember the story of the fisherman who caught a magic fish. He and his wife were granted three wishes. But they wished before they thought. First the fisherman's hungry wife wished for a pudding. It appeared. Then, the fisherman, angry with his wife for wasting a wish, wished that the pudding would be stuck on her nose. And then, of course, they had to use up their last wish to get the pudding unstuck from her nose.

Naturally, you wouldn't be that stupid! But before you invoke the power of prayer, be sure that what you pray for is what you need, and not just what you think you want. Prayer is powerful stuff. Prayer, and peace, faith, hope, love, kindness, honor and caring are all God's Tools of Power, and he gave them to us to use as we see fit. Even if we aren't quite sure what to do with them yet, they are wonderful gifts, and will guide us to our life purpose. No matter what your religious beliefs are, it is all-important to be at one with God, for the love you feel for God will be returned to you tenfold.

**DAY**
**4**
**MONDAY**

# AFFIRMATION:
# I'VE GOT WHAT IT TAKES.

#1.  Today is Monday, the start of a brand new week. Remember to keep cleaning your teeth with the toothbrush in the opposite hand.

#2.  Start the day with a smile and a cheery word.  Stretch your body.  Look forward to what you will be experiencing this week - even though it's a Monday morning.  Look forward to the changes that are about to happen. You are in for some nice surprises.  Go with the super-flow!

#3.  Today, whenever you have a negative thought, turn it right around on the spot into a positive thought.  This will teach you to look at the brighter side of a situation, no matter how bad it seems.  Put a rubber band around your wrist (not too tight) and for the next five days, every time you become discontented about something snap the band as hard as you can - this will remind you to think positive thoughts.

**A.M. Real Thought (Morning Break):** *I am going to be nice to everybody this week.*

#4. For lunch today, eat with somebody different, someone that you don't know very well who may be sitting alone. If you have taken your lunch to work, share it.

#5. Try to see whatever you are doing this afternoon in a different, more positive light. Sing or hum to yourself. Get in the mood; remember the old songs that you used to sing.

#6. It is time to think about taking some kind of evening class, something different, something you have always wanted to do but thought you couldn't. Sign up for a semester.

#7. If you have a disagreement today or any other day this week, try to see the other person's point of view. Step into his or her shoes for a while.

#8. For the next three days, for every kind deed you do for someone else, do a big or small one for yourself.

#9. Keep in your mind that a stranger is a friend whom you have yet to make. New friends attract new happenings.

#10. Tonight, turn off the TV. Start to read a good book, or a bad one - or play some silly games. Every half hour or so, say something nice to someone even if you have to call them. If you can find no one to say it to, say it to yourself.

**P.M. Real Thought:** *Those around you may not like the things that you are doing this week.* Remember that it is *their* problem, not yours. You are doing this for *you.*

#11. If you live in the country, go to the city. If you live in the city, go to the country. Make plans tonight to do this sometime within the next two weeks. Tell yourself why you can, instead of why you can't – and get excited about it!

#12. Be in bed before 10:00 p.m. Get a good night's sleep, as you will be taking a different route to work or wherever you have to go tomorrow.

**Repeat Affirmation: I've got what it takes.**

# EXPLANATION FOR DAY FOUR

#1. To maintain your program of change this week, it is important to remind yourself daily that you are trying to approach life in a different way. That is why you need to keep brushing your teeth with the opposite hand, as a daily reminder that you are changing this week. Have you noticed you're getting more comfortable with it?

#2. You may think that your smiles are only for other people, that you are "putting on a front" for public display. This is not true. You smile for yourself - your most important audience. Starting your day with a smile, even if you are only smiling to yourself when you wake up in the morning, will help set the mood for the entire day.

More people die of heart attacks on Monday morning than any other time. It is important to find something to look forward to before you get out of bed, some reason to get up and start your day. If you can't think of a single positive thing in your real life, then invent something positive to do during the day - and then get up and actually do it! Make the most of *every* day.

#3. Your brain only knows what you tell it. If you say "I can't", then your brain believes you. So change that thought to "I can". Remind yourself of this with a snap of your rubber band every time you find yourself veering toward "I can't." The slight pain you feel with the snap of the rubber band will bring you back to your senses.

Everyone knows that optimists see a glass half-full and pessimists see the glass half-empty. But no one ever bothers to point out that they are both right - only the optimist is happy! Be the optimist, and make each day brighter.

**A.M. Real Thought:** This is not going to be easy - a whole week of being nice? After the first day, though, you will realize that when you are pleasant, others will be pleasant in return. Your behavior comes back to you. Maybe you will be scorned by one person you are nice to, but sure enough, someone else will be nice back to you down the line. And, what is more important, you will *feel* nice. Isn't that nice? Isn't that *great*?

#4. This week, you will be reaching out to many different people. You may find you like their behavior and customs, or you may also find that you are comfortable in your own ways. No matter what, you have gained something by sharing with them. Life is a flow of energy; if you only give, or only take, you are refusing life itself. Give a little, take a little, win a little, lose a little, go with the flow. By sharing a meal with someone new, you will learn more about yourself and about the world and people around you.

#5. Try to find the good in everything you do, no matter how routine. Every task is important - what would the world be like without clean floors, or neatly typed documents, or a friendly word on the telephone? You leave your mark on everything you do and touch. Find some enjoyment in your work and your personal touch. Feel valuable!

We all have music inside of us, but we must remember to let it out once in awhile! Young people seem to sing more and listen to music more frequently, but remember, you are as young as you choose to be!

#6. One of the best ways to open the door to new experiences in your life is to take lessons, in anything that fascinates you. You will appreciate that language or artistic technique or writing style even more after you know something about it. And your self-esteem will grow with this increased knowledge - you will feel like you are truly growing and accomplishing new things. Plus, these classes are something to really look forward to. Not only do you learn more about what interests you, but you meet new people who also share in your interests. Don't put off signing up for a class or two. You will be glad you did.

#7. Putting yourself into someone else's shoes can be tough. You may not be able to understand their opposing point of view, but try. Remember there are really three sides to every story - yours, theirs, and the one nobody thought of .

#8. If you are a kind person, it is easy to do a kind deed for some one else, even for a stranger. Then why is it so hard to do something kind for yourself? Do you think you don't deserve it? Wrong! Are you too proud to accept a favor, even from yourself? Go ahead, do something nice for yourself. Not an indulgence, like hot fudge sundaes, but something that will make your life easier. Take a nap, cut yourself some slack in household chores. Back off on the demands you make on yourself, and give yourself a break.

#9. "Xenophobia" is a fancy word for hating strangers. Too often, we are wary of people who speak different languages and have different customs. Television and travel have changed some of this fear, but it is still hard to accept somebody from a completely different environment. Strangers are, by definition, strange, but you'll find that once you get to know someone new, you will be amazed at how much you have in common.

#10. There is nothing wrong with watching some TV, but we get so wrapped up with what is on television that we forget that there are other things to do. Reading a book forces your imagination to go to work - it's good exercise for your brain. Games also provoke your imagination and your wits – a good anti-Alzheimers' exercise! Did you feel the creative energy this evening? And did saying something nice every half hour get the good vibrations flowing?

**P.M. Real Thought:** One of the hardest things to overcome, when you are eager to change, is the limitations others impose on you. You must be strong - if those around you want to stop your growth for any reason, you have to realize that it is their problem, not yours. Too often, we live for other people. This is your time to change, and you will be surprised, but they will come around in the end and change with you.

#11. Change of viewpoint plus change of surroundings equals change of reality. Taking a trip to the city or country expands your horizons and opens up new worlds. You may find you like it better where you are, or you might decide there is something appealing in moving.

#12. You need a good night's sleep in order to feel fresh and confident enough to fulfill what destiny has in store for you. Too many people think of nights as a time to go over the worries of the day. But bed should be the place where you can be alone with your soul, or your soulmate. Make it a habit, when you turn out the light, to tune out anything that troubles you. Imagine that your bed is a fortress. You can pull up the drawbridge, and all the problems of the day will have to stay outside. Don't worry - they will still be there in the morning, and you can confront them then – if you still want to..

# YOU GET WHAT YOU THINK YOU DESERVE

I once knew two brothers. One of them believed he could always win and the other believed that he could not. They ended up both being right

At a very early age in my life, I decided that I was dumb. Because I had no self-esteem, I thought that everybody was better than I. I fed off the worry and fear that surrounded my insecurity, my intense desire to be liked and to do well in school. I played the clown, allowed and encouraged people to take advantage of me and trample on my ego. I made excuses and jokes about being at the bottom of the class, where I deserved to be. I did these personal put-downs to make other people laugh. I didn't even think that I was worthy of a seat on the bus. I'd stand up so others could sit down, not for good manners, but just so I could get the recognition and a "Thank you" from the person who took my seat.

I didn't know it then, but putting myself down had become a habit. I thought like a loser, and was a loser. I remember a boy who cried in elementary school because he got a math problem wrong. I didn't understand why he was crying at the time. What was the big deal - I got *all* my math problems wrong! I never expected to do any better. And no one ever told me I could do better. Now I know that to change for the better you have to say "I can" and "I will." As a child, no one told me that.

Life was rough then, though. The first seven years of my life were spent dodging German bombs that were dropped daily on London. My father was doing war work - 12 hours in a factory and another 12 hours as a fire-fighter. Many times in a week, he would come home covered in blood from digging people out. The meaning of life was simple: try to survive. At Christmas, I'd get an apple or an orange and maybe a book with someone else's name in it, that they had received for Christmas last year. We were lucky to have a roof over our heads and something to eat. I never knew what I wanted to do in life. I never knew that I *could* do anything in life. I was scared, afraid of change, and even in poor health, with horrible migraines.

Years later, I discovered that many of my problems in school, and much of the basis of low self-esteem, came from me being "learning impaired." I was somewhat dyslexic and suffered from a short attention span. We didn't know this then. I just blamed myself for being stupid. Every night I prayed to be better and smarter, but nothing changed.

While it seemed like tragedy at the time, now I see that my dyslexia was not such a terrible curse. Because I couldn't learn from the way teachers taught in the regular classes, I never was programmed into society's traditional ways of thinking and believing. Today, I think that's a blessing! Like many disasters, it had a silver lining, because once I realized that I was learning-impaired, I was able to learn how to overcome my so-called limitations.

I learned how to turn my lemons into lemonade by changing my attitude. You can learn this too. It has become common practice these days to wallow in self-pity and blame everything on someone else - the victim has been used and abused, and thus has the "right" to use and abuse others. TV talk shows highlight failure as if it were a badge of honor, and give people free reign to whine about what they wanted and should have had. This is a decade of "free lunches", but what a price to pay in human dignity when instead of accepting the fact that life is rough and then *moving on in a positive way*, we dwell on the negative.

It doesn't matter what you've gone through in the past. The bottom line is that you and only you can turn your life around and make it better. It is a slow process to rebuild your confidence and learn how to embrace life fully, but it can be done. I did it. When I left home to go into the army, my migraines disappeared and I saw that I could live my life in a different way. All I had to do was make the decision to change. I began to tap the infinite power of positive being. The scary feeling that I originally felt became exciting, and the light at the end of the tunnel grew brighter.

I say "positive being" because just thinking positive is not enough. Everybody deserves the best, but only a certain consciousness and way of being attracts the best. This Seven Day Program is designed to raise that level of consciousness and establish that way of being in you. It's a big step in the right direction. You have to learn to *expect* a better way of life. Though it seems that some individuals are "born lucky" and that fortune smiles on them, they actually expect to do well and have success. We impose our own limitations, and it is up to us to get rid of these limitations and reach for the stars.

Learning to accept, whether it is help, support, love or success, is our birthright. Imagine a newborn baby rejecting help because he doesn't deserve it or need it. He would die. You die a little, spiritually, emotionally, intellectually, when you refuse to accept the best. Replace "why me?" with "why not me?", and never look for reasons to reject your rewards. Be the king of your personal castle - know your true worth, and wallow in it.

**DAY**
**5**

**TUESDAY**

# Affirmation: I like being happy.

#1. Sometime today go to a movie, a different kind of movie, even if you have to rearrange your normal schedule. Pick a movie that you normally wouldn't dream of seeing. Plan what movie you will see as you take a different route to work or your daily errands. Today is a day to explore. Look for things that you haven't noticed before.

#2. Get an "I love you" card and send it to someone whom you really love. Tell someone whom you haven't told lately that you love him or her.

#3. Today is "Get Rid of a Bad Habit" day. You are going to replace a bad habit with a good habit. Decide which habits are good and bad, and then begin replacing the bad with the good. Start with the bad habit that bothers you the most.

#4. At lunch time, call a special friend and listen, really listen to every word he or she says. Try to hear what might be bothering your friend. Don't judge him or her. Just listen. Keep your advice to yourself unless your friend asks for it.

**A.M. Real Thought:** *Trust your intuitive thoughts and live by them.* Everybody has some inner psychic ability.

#5. Today is the day to tap into your desires. Make a written list of all of the things that you would like to have and do with your life. Be somewhat realistic, but also let your mind stretch into your dreams.

#6. It is time to think about doing some physical exercise, if you are not doing any. Pick something that you like and stick with it on a regular basis. You will make new friends and get healthier at the same time. Anything will do, as long as you do it!

**P.M. Real Thought:** *Love yourself first. Then extend that love to other people.* Now you are learning how the flow of love works.

#7. Spend time this evening with children. If you don't have any, find someone else's. Talk to them, have fun with them. Think about being a big brother or sister to some child who doesn't have anybody. Make sure this is quality time, for everyone involved. It's best not to eat junk food, drink or smoke during this exercise.

#8. Before you go to sleep write yourself a letter on what you think about yourself and how you want to improve your life. Tomorrow, mail it to yourself (no e-mail). When it comes back to you, read it, date it and put it in a safe place. Repeat this on a weekly basis for three months.

**Repeat affirmation: I like being happy.**

# EXPLANATION FOR DAY FIVE

#1. Movies, like all art forms, have a deep effect on our consciousness. You spend an hour or so living someone else's life. During this week of change, you are trying to expand your consciousness. Go see a type of movie you never watch - if you like tear jerkers, go to an action adventure movie. If you like car chases, try a more artistically challenging movie – and become part of it..

Most people go to work the same way every day. It is a habit, getting somewhere as soon as possible. Going to work by a different route will change your vibrations. This may frustrate you, but seeing things from a different perspective will open you up to a different view of this new day. Did you look around you today? Did you notice the different architecture and scenery? Even if it took you a few extra minutes to get to work today, you picked up something on this trip that will be beneficial to you in the long run.

#2. Buying a card for someone gets you thinking about whom you love. Is your love a secret. Or are you sharing with this person the wonderful gift of your love? You might want to send two or three cards to show how much you care, and how much they are appreciated.

#3. We all have habits. Some of them are good, like brushing our teeth, paying our bills, calling our mothers. Make a list of your habits, with a good column and bad column. Think of some good habits you'd like to acquire and add them to the list. Whenever you find yourself acting out a habit from the bad side of the list, replace it with one of the good ones. They say it takes 21 days to break a bad habit, so try doing this for 21 days. Only work on one of your bad habits at a time - you will be more effective that way. If you have trouble identifying your bad habits, ask your partner or friends. They always know!

#4. So few people really listen. And yet, that is the only way we ever learn anything. Very often, the kindest thing you can do for a friend is to listen. We all have a need to "get it off our chest", and talking about our problems is a way of healing - that's why the psychiatrists earn the big bucks. You don't have to provide answers. Your friend will discover his or her own answers while talking to you, or may just feel relieved to have shared problems with a caring friend. And you will feel good too for being a good friend.

**A.M. Real Thought:** There is only one person who knows what is right for you in the long run and that is you. If you listen - really listen - to your intuition, you may make some mistakes, but you will never go wrong in the long run if you trust yourself.

#5. If you don't know what you want to do or be, how can you do or be it? Be specific; plan out the house you want, the daily routine you desire, the right love relationship, the money, the joys and challenges that would make your life so much better. Don't sit around waiting for a lottery win, because you could wait forever. Get into positive action, and positive being *now*.

#6. Exercise is the single most important thing you can do for your body, your mind and your spirit. I guarantee if will help clear the darkest of moods. The trick to joyful exercise is finding something you enjoy doing - walking, playing a sport, walking on a treadmill while watching TV - anything that is fun that you can look forward to. Make a commitment and stick to it.

**P.M. Real Thought:** If you do not love yourself, how can you love another? Love is trusting; do you trust yourself? Love is believing; do you believe in yourself? Love is giving; can you give of yourself? Love is finding another person wonderful; you are wonderful.

#7. Children (and puppies and kittens for that matter) are the natural wonder of our lives. Being with them makes you remember what is really important: *being alive* in God's world. If you see life through the eyes of a child, you will once again see that life is a miracle, that trees are beautiful and that there is joy in running and playing, and that tomorrow is too far away to worry about. This is an exercise in connecting. Don't be in such a hurry to grow up – be a child for a while, play and be happy.

#8. Putting your thoughts into words often gives you a different perspective on things. Writing them down and reading them again days or months later leads to answers you would never have anticipated. It is very important that you mail these letters to yourself. The anticipation of reading them adds to the magic. Read them all again, in order, three months later to see how far you've come. If things are still the same, then obviously you need to do a bit more changing.

# Enough is Never Enough

A long time ago, when I was living in New York City, I was seeing a woman who had a good job, who traveled, who loved animals, who was an all-around decent person. But her personal life was a mess. Nothing ever seemed to go right. Nothing ever pleased her. Despite the positive things in her life, she was sunk in a rut of unhappiness. The vibrations surrounding her were all wrong, and she didn't know how to change that.

One evening, after going out to dinner and then back to her place, we had a long discussion about the way she was living her life. And then it struck me what was wrong! I asked her if she would let me paint her small apartment. "You pick the color, I'll do all the work," I told her. So she bought the paint, and I did the work.

After a couple of days, the place was transformed. Not only did that paint perk her up and change the negative vibrations, but it actually changed her life. That simple change - a new coat of paint - started the ball rolling. She took a trip to Japan, where she met a man who coincidentally lived across the street from her in New York. After a magic courtship, they married. Not only did she find love, but she found wealth as well, for he was a millionaire.

Her happiness and good vibrations spread out and affected other people too. It is amazing to watch this kind of ripple effect. And it can all start with something as simple as a new paint job. Sometimes it is a smile or a good deed that will get you out of your rut. This Seven Day program is designed to help you look at life in a new way, to get you thinking about the future. It will help you realize that it is O.K. to want more; it is O.K. to move forward, just like my friend realized that it was O.K. to want a change in her life.

The one thing in life that everybody wants is more - more money, more health, more love - and more life! We want prosperity, a sense of well-being. Some people are truly happy with a life of simplicity, but the majority of people have desires and dreams that they want to strive for, a measure of prosperity they want to attain. There is nothing wrong with wanting more - in fact, you could even say it is a blessing. There is no need to stay stuck in a life of unhappiness, a life of wanting and waiting for something to happen. This book will help you to realize that it is good to want to change your life and to strive for success and happiness, but the most important thing to remember is this: if you have not planned for this success, if you have not worked for it, then it can all turn into disaster.

There is a Persian curse that says, "May all your desires be instantly granted." Winning the lottery, hitting the jackpot - these are ways to prosperity, sure, but are they realistic for most people? You may think you want to be instantly rich, but think a little harder - would you know how to handle this wealth? Would you feel like you had earned this prosperity? Think of all the time and money you are wasting if this is your way to prosperity. Prosperity comes to those who are open to change, to those who realize that we live in a universe of staggering dimensions and unlimited possibilities. The key is understanding that the means to prosperity, for striving to get "enough", lie in *you*.

From the moment you are born, you are in business for yourself. Prosperity is available to you from Day One, whether you realize it or not. The only barriers to you striving for happiness and success are the barriers you throw in your own path. Your heart, your brain, your soul, is what determines whether you will be unhappy in your lot or will seek to change your life. It's all there in your make-up - you just need a kick in the pants sometimes to see it. God supplies the birds with everything they need to build a nest. He just doesn't build the nest for them.

Once you see that you possess the keys to your own prosperity, you can go about making it happen in your life. Never limit yourself As you cannot escape the business of living, if you want prosperity, you cannot escape the business of business. The best way to find prosperity is to find something you enjoy doing, and then work hard at it.

A friend of mine in England had a successful career in the newspaper business, but he hated every minute of it. "I'm dying in this job," he would say. Then one day he got up the courage to do what he'd always wanted to do - start a band and play the saxophone. He had been afraid he might starve, but these fears were never realized. He is not super-rich, but now he is happy - and so is his family. Remember, prosperity does not have to always mean money. One can prosper in happiness and inner peace as well.

A lot of people, like my friend in England, dislike their jobs. But if you hate your job, do you really think that you will be able to prosper in it? Changing your attitude about work, doing the best you can with every detail, will bring about recognition, increased pay, promotions. Very rarely do you find anyone who has been promoted for disliking his job. If you take a safe job because of the benefits, all you will have are those benefits. If you feel content and prosperous with that, then fine. But if you want more out of work, be willing to do one of two things: learn to love your job, or find one that you like better. Many people have two or three careers in one lifetime. There's no reason to get stuck.

Loving and having fun with the work you do will bring prosperity to you in ways you would never think possible. You do not have to accept a life of poverty and unhappiness. You do not have to be stuck in a rut. Just because some one pays you for disability is no reason to see yourself as disabled.

If you want to be a winner, you have to tell yourself it is all right to be rich. It is all right to want security. It is all right to accept the wealth of the world that God wants to share with everyone who is open enough to receive it.

And, after you have worked hard to change your life and your attitude and prosperity has come your way, don't forget to be appreciative of this and give a little of it back. Share the wealth of the world and of the universe with others. Life and prosperity will flow through you - don't block the flow. When you get what you think you want, when you attain a level of prosperity that makes you happy (and if you follow this program, you will), realize that it is important to find something else worth striving for. It is human nature to need goals in order to be happy - even, in order to live. Ambition keeps us going, and effort keeps us interested in life. That is why enough is never enough.

And that's O.K.!

DAY

# 6

**WEDNESDAY**

## Affirmation: I like being me.

#1. Think about the fact that today is the first day of the rest of your life. Make this day very special. It's the time of your awakening. The first thing you do this morning is to pray about the thing that is really bothering you the most. Then spend five minutes quietly listening to the answer.

#2. Be prepared to start feeling different, whatever form it may take. Just don't panic.

**A.M. Real Thought:** *My life is in divine order and I expect it to get better each day.*

#3. Today is the day that you only live for you. This day, nothing else exists. You live one second at a time, leaving the past behind and being *yourself* in the here and now. Be kind, be nice, be funny, be happy with yourself. You can play today. Do what you have to do, but do it in the best possible way.

#4. This is a day of being aware of yourself, taking time to enjoy being who you are. There's a different you developing; get to know this new you. Look in a different mirror. Does it show? Look closer. Take time to absorb everything that you see. Don't get hung up on wrinkles or blemishes. See the true beauty which is beginning to shine through.

#5. Spend lunchtime with someone you like, and say all the nice things you can think of - make sure that you mean everything you say. It might be embarrassing at first, but feel pleased at being able to make some one feel good.

#6. Sometime this afternoon think of something nice to buy yourself next weekend. Remember you are still taking the day one second at a time and living in the here and now, but think for a moment about something that will improve you and make you happy in the future. Maybe a self-help tape or book, or some clothes. Just plant the seed. When you are in the store, what is right for you will jump out.

#7.  Say to yourself over and over again, "Each day in every way, I feel happier and happier."

#8.  I hope that you have found time this week for some kind of sexual activity that is pleasing to you and hurts nobody else. (Children doing this workout should postpone this part for a few years!)

#9.  Make a list of your own Ten Commandments and start to live by them.  Really think before you write – remember, it's your life.

#10.  All day today, keep telling yourself "I feel great!"  Say it again, "I feel great!"

**P.M. Real Thought:** *Am I in the habit of smiling more yet?*

#11.  When driving home from work or errands today, remember to use your safety belt.  Whenever you are in a car, be in the habit of using safety belts.  The life you save could be your own.

#12.  Before you go to bed, fill up the bathtub with warm water. Pour some nice smelling stuff into it, light some candles, put on some love theme music and climb in.  Stay there relaxing for at least 20 minutes.  Think good thoughts.  Be at peace and connect with your spirit.  This is a gift to yourself.

#13.  Before you go to sleep tonight, sit quietly by yourself. Close your eyes, think of someone  you love and swallow.  Did the swallow stick in your throat?  I bet it didn't.  Now again, close your eyes, think of someone who has hurt you or whom you don't like and swallow.  If that lump sticks in your throat, you had better forgive that person before you go to sleep tonight. And don't forget to forgive your old self, if you are choking on something you did in the past.

**Repeat affirmation: I like being me.**

# EXPLANATION FOR DAY SIX

#1. You are very precious. There is no one in the world the same as you. You are one of a kind, unique. Did you honor yourself today? Did you call a truce today from your daily woes, not letting that little negative voice inside get to you? How did it feel to really listen to your true self? If you really listen, you will eventually understand. It is then that you will be able to make the changes you've been working on, and things will start to fall into place.

#2. If you want to change, you have to be prepared to accept this change. You will actually start feeling different. That's the first sign that there will be great changes in your life.

The scary thing about changing is that you can't predict what will happen. If life were predictable, though, it would be very dull. You need to think toward the future and toward this change - clinging to the past is like refusing to leave a sinking ship. The trick is to run out and embrace this change, and greet the future with joy and faith. Your ship will come in, and give you the trip of your life!

**A.M. Real Thought:** Think about the deeper meaning of Divine Order. What does it mean to you? A place for everything and everything in its place? Or is it the grand scheme that lies under everything that happens in this world? Thinking about such things occasionally will calm your spirit and enable you to see the greater truths. Being at peace and knowing that everything will be all right is the answer to all of life's experiences.

#3. The present is all we really own. It's O.K. to fill it with dreams and memories, if you want to - but don't forget you are making tomorrow's memories with every second. The more you enjoy the present, the happier your memories will be.

#4. You looked into a different mirror today to avoid looking at the image you are used to seeing. When you look in the mirror, you shouldn't criticize your body. Maybe a few things could use touching up, but the real reason for this exercise was to see if you noticed a difference in yourself - such as an air of confidence or a sense of excitement – the good stuff!

#5. Friendship is precious and important. Sharing a pleasant time, such as a meal, with a person you like will help cement your friendship and will be like a bright island in your day, something you can look forward to. At lunch today did you talk about all the good things that you share with your friend and not dwell on the negative?

#6. Thinking about the little gifts that you are going to give yourself is as much fun as actually buying them! Once again, we need to have things to look forward to throughout the day. Did you think about gifts that will improve your mind, help your confidence, educate you in some way? Self-improvement is the gift that keeps on giving. It is money spent that will never be wasted. Education is the only gift that will last forever. It's all yours; it can't be borrowed, stolen, or broken.

#7. Are you getting the hang of feeling happy? It is important to enforce the habit of happiness. Whenever you feel sorry for yourself or feel the urge to wallow in some sort of misery, stop, snap the elastic band around your wrist, and say "I AM HAPPY!" You will be amazed at how you can snap yourself out of being sad.

#8. We are physical beings, and should not ignore our sexuality. Repressing sexual urges only leads to trouble - your anger and hostility will creep up in other areas of your life. If you act responsibly as a sexual being, you will feel better about yourself and about the world around you.

#9. Did you write out your list of Ten Commandments today? You should memorize these personal commandments and remind yourself of them daily. Everyone needs a personal code of honor, a set of commandments that will enrich and strengthen your life. Rejoice in the pride and strength you feel when you follow these rules.

#10. Has anyone ever said to you that you look tired, or sick, or sad? Did you actually feel tired or sick when they told you that? The same thing happens when you look in the mirror and say "I feel tired today." Guess what - you are going to feel tired! It works the opposite way, though. If you tell yourself you feel and look great, then you will.

**P.M. Real Thought:** Remember what I said about forming habits? Smiling is one of the most beautiful habits you can have. It blesses everyone it touches.

#11. I have a friend who believes that if she carries an umbrella, it won't rain. Buckling your seatbelt will not prevent an accident, but it could save your life if you do have an accident. Look after what is precious to you - your life!

#12. Water has a magical effect - it soothes us, makes us feel safe. When you soak in a hot tub of water, it is as though you and the water become one. To add to this pleasure, you can try aromatherapy, adding the scent of balsam for relaxation, rosemary for remembrance, or any other kind of scent you like. Adding candlelight and music intensifies your magical experience, and helps you connect with your source..

#13. How long did it take you tonight to swallow that lump in your throat? Did you have to stop thinking about the person who hurt you and think about someone else in order to finally swallow? Don't live with those lumps. Get the poison out of your system by forgiving and forgetting the bad that has been done to you - and the bad that you have done to others. Put it behind you this very night, and look forward to your clean new day tomorrow, and cleaner days to come. It's a spiritual renewal.

# LEARNING TO LISTEN - TO YOURSELF

Most of us know how to operate a car. When we drive, we direct the car, steering to the right or to the left, going fast or slow. We maintain our cars with fuel, water, oil, etc., or they will break down, and when we are driving, we stick to the rules of the road for safety's sake.

Think of your body this way as well, as a vessel containing your spirit, like your car contains your body. When your car breaks down, you take it to a mechanic. When your body breaks down, you take it to a doctor. But sometimes the problem is with the *way* you drive, or the road you have chosen, not your actual vehicle. And in our lives, sometimes our problems have nothing to do with the food we eat, the exercise we do, or the rest we get. We know how to keep our bodies healthy, but do we realize how important it is to keep our *minds* and *spirits* healthy as well? And do we realize how important it is to see that our minds and bodies work together to create a healthy, happy, whole person?

Mind, body and spirit are intimately connected, in ways so profound it can be difficult to understand. Our interior world is a mysterious and complex place. I believe that every day we have to contend with not only our conscious mind, but with both our subconscious and our powerful, true Inner Selves. Your conscious mind is what you are doing or thinking about doing. Your subconscious is everything you have had to deal with in the past, just simmering under your consciousness. And your Inner Self is your spirit, your mediator, the force that tries to make sense of all the things you have experienced.

Twenty-four hours a day, seven days a week, 365 days a year, you are under the influence of these forces. Your subconscious and conscious mind work through thoughts, and your Inner Self works through feelings which turn into thoughts. Your Inner Self understands the true nature of your soul, better than your conscious self does. When you have trouble or chaos in life, it is often because you are not listening to your Inner Self – only that little inside voice that leads you astray..

This chapter, and this program, are really all about listening to your Inner Self, knowing that your physical health and your happiness are dependent on making sure that you listen to what your Inner Self is saying. This is the positive self that guides you, that tells you which direction to take your body, what road to follow. It is the self that will help you conquer cravings, give up smoking, keep you fit and trim, find love - in essence, your whole physical being is tied up with your inner psychic being.

The relationship between your physical self and your Inner Self is so profound that you can actually feel *psychic* problems in your life as *physical* problems. Listening to your Inner Self is sometimes as simple as paying attention to your physical self and what it is trying to tell you about your life. Such as:

If you wake up with a stiff neck, look for the person or situation that is acting like "a pain in the neck."

If you have hemorrhoids, who in your life is "the pain in the butt?"

Stomach pains are usually a sign of trying to digest new situations or of old ones that are not resolved.

Sore knees can indicate ego problems.

Money problems can be felt as back pain.

Desmond Morris, author of *The Human Animal*, made an interesting observation about the intelligence of horses in his book, *Horsewatching*: "Horses know everything they need to know about being horses - which is more than humans do." I believe, though, that we really can know everything we need to know about being human, that it is all there inside of us. We just have to be able to listen to what our bodies tell us and what our Inner Selves tell us, and then we will find the way to an improved life.

Many people feel cravings - cravings for drugs, alcohol or excess amounts of food. What is really happening is that they are craving endorphins - the "feel-good" chemicals of the brain. If we listen to our Inner Selves, though, and to our bodies, we can find natural ways to overcome these cravings and make our lives better and more interesting. Simple exercise releases those same endorphins into our brains. Just climbing a flight of stairs faster than you usually do will release those endorphins.

People who are trying to diet, or to change bad habits like smoking, taking drugs, or drinking too much alcohol should also spend more time listening to their bodies. What is it they really crave? Is it more rest, more stimulation, or more love? It usually isn't the actual drug, or the drink, but something else. If you ever feel a craving for something like this, try to meditate. Concentrate on how your body really feels, what your mind is trying to tell you. Try to ride the wave of instant gratification, wait out these cravings. Take a nap, have a drink of water, eat only a little food and then wait ten minutes (that's how long it takes your stomach to get the message that you've just eaten something).

The ten minute rule is a good one for many things. Exercise your self discipline by saying "I'll have a cigarette (or a piece of candy, or a drink, or whatever) in ten minutes." Anyone can wait that long for something, if you really want it And half the time, you'll find you don't want your drink or candy or cigarette after ten minutes.

If you really listen to your positive Inner Self, you will find out what your body needs. Usually it is more activity, like exercise. The normal body was meant to exercise. Next time you are in a bad, dull mood, just try jumping up and down a few times - and see how much better you feel! This exercise releases pent-up energy, shakes off negative vibrations, and balances your aura. This is your mind and body working together to give you peace and restore balance. If you listen to your Inner Self, you are less likely to suffer from the boredom that plagues many people. Most people who are bored refuse to listen to themselves, to their Inner Self that wants variety and activity. Taking a class, joining a reading group, riding a bike, feeding the ducks, helping underprivileged children, are all things that will alleviate boredom. The only thing that is holding you back from enjoying life is yourself - break through those blocks that are silencing your inner desire to have fun! Be your own Healer!

Listening to yourself is much more than just sensing that your body needs rest, exercise, and a little fun. You need to spend a little time alone with yourself each day and realize that your psyche is picking up messages at this time. Most people get confused or scared of this psychic power - they think it's mumbo jumbo, fortune telling. Really, it is your sixth sense, which, when used correctly, powerfully works with your other five senses. You may call it intuition, or imagination, but everyone has a certain amount of this psychic power inside of them. The key is tapping into this power and using it to help guide you in your choices.

My suggestions for how to do this are simple - try meditation, prayer, focusing on happy and kind thoughts, seeing the good and not the bad in life. Really basic stuff here, but potentially quite powerful.

If you get anything out of this program, I hope it is this: that the power to change your life is within yourself. All you have to do is listen to your body, listen to your Inner Self, be ready to tap into your own psychic abilities.

And don't be afraid to embrace what you hear.

**DAY**

**7**

**THURSDAY**

# AFFIRMATION:
# I HAVE ABUNDANT ENERGY.

#1.  Once you are awake, stick your head into a pillow and let out two loud screams.  Then do it again!

**A.M. Real Thought:** *How do I feel?*  Answer yourself aloud, twice, and be honest.

#2.  Before you go out into the world, look around the place you live in. What needs doing?  Maybe some painting or changing the curtains?  Look for something light and easy to do, and do it within the next four weeks. Think about it on your way to where you are going.  Make mental or written notes.  And get enthusiastic about it!

#3. Think about giving a nice surprise to someone today, and do it. It is up to you what kind of surprise. Think about the type of response you might expect back from them. A lot of people do not know how to take. You are just spreading some joy.

#4. If you are into a routine of sitting in the same place at home, or at work, change seats. Sleep upside down in your bed, with your feet at the head of the bed. Change as much as you can on this last day. Soon you will be back to some of your old tricks, but also some of the new will have rubbed off on you. Rearrange some of the furniture in your home, or even in your space at work. Be creative. And do it today.

**P.M. Real Thought:** *Are you still finding fault in what other people do?*

#5. Make a list of the things that you like about yourself, and make a list of the things that you don't like about yourself. Save these lists. Do this once a month for a year. Date them and save them. At the end of the year, compare the lists.

#6.  Remember that the meaning of what you say is the response you get back.  So choose your words wisely.

#7.  Buy yourself a hat.  Just spend a few dollars if you are short of money.  And make sure that you wear and enjoy it!  Be different.

#8.  Pretend you are a child again.  Lie on the grass and look at what Mother Nature has given you; the sky, birds, even bugs.  Look at the world as if you've never seen it before - and as if you were just three feet tall.  Connect with what is real.  It will be fun!

#9.  Share what you have learned this week with somebody else who needs it.  But don't expect them to be as enthusiastic as you are, because they may not be motivated.

#10.  Take everything off your dresser or bathroom counter except one thing.  Then really look at that one thing.  Think about where it was made, its use, and what it means to you.

#11. When you are in bed, say to yourself three times, "What others think of me is none of my business." Isn't that great? Fall asleep with that thought on your mind. You are being set free.

# EXPLANATION FOR DAY 7

#1. You will be amazed at how much better you can feel after a good scream or two. It lets out all the pent-up frustration and anger that has been building up for a long time. Don't be scared to do this. It is important to get negative thoughts and energy out of your system every once in awhile. So scream away - into the pillow, please, so no one hears you and calls 911!

**A.M. Real Thought:** How do you *really* feel? Don't just answer "fine" - most of us rarely feel just fine. Ask yourself this question on a regular basis, and answer out loud. You'll get a more honest answer if you hear it out loud, and you will be more apt to pay attention to your response.

#2. Sometimes it is easier to change your surroundings than it is to change yourself. Think how different you feel when you go on vacation. Make your home into your own private hideaway.

#3. The act of giving not only makes the receiver happy; it also makes you happy to think of the pleasure your gift brings. Aren't you lucky to be a person who is able to give? And when you understand the joy of giving, you'll be able to receive gracefully as well. That is the true meaning of "It is better to give than to receive."

#4. If you want to change your life (and you do, since you are completing this program), you must start by changing little things. First the chair, then the sofa - then your life! If you don't like the outcome of these experiments, then put your furniture back where it was, or start sleeping in bed the way you used to.

**P.M. Real Thought:** Don't find fault with others. From now on, try to understand their differences instead of attacking them for being different.

#5. Which of your lists that you did today was longer? Is it the negative list? Then you've either got a lot of things to change about your life, or you need to look at yourself in a whole new way. Are those negatives really true? Be kind to yourself, and emphasize the good that I know is in you. If you have learned anything from this program, your likes should outbalance the dislikes by far!

#6. We humans have a deep need to be understood. That's why we communicate with other people. By "understood," we almost always mean being liked and loved. But if you don't think before you speak and choose hurtful or inappropriate words or an off-putting tone, you may be misunderstood. If you project a positive attitude, and choose your words accordingly when you speak, then people will much less likely to misunderstand you, and much more likely to like you.

#7. Have you ever noticed that people, even strangers, are more likely to comment on your appearance if you are wearing a hat? Hats seem to attract attention. They give you a new image. Ask yourself why you picked the hat that you bought today. Is it a conservative hat, or something more daring? Did you choose a baseball hat because you are in a sporting mood, or a straw hat because it reminds you of going on vacation?

#8. Children are fascinated with the world because everything is new to them. They are free and uninhibited and have not been programmed to society's ways. We can all recapture this sense of wonder and find joy in simple things? Did you notice this magic today when you looked at the world through a child's eyes?

#9. Those who succeed in life and don't share their knowledge and experience get very little pleasure out of their accomplishments. What most of us need and want is not someone to share our sadness, but someone to rejoice in our victories. So do yourself a favor, and share what you have learned. Some people may resist your ideas, but if you are able to help one person just a little bit, then all your hard work and accomplishments will mean even more. Don't look for praise – your good deeds will be blessed and returned in other ways.

#10. Housekeeping columnist Heloise says that if you leave a sock on the dresser long enough, your subconscious mind will think it belongs there and you will stop seeing it. How many things in your house have you stopped seeing? The Japanese believe in putting out one object at a time and really looking at it. Then, when you have stopped actually noticing it, put it away and try something new. Stop taking things for granted. Live consciously, and be aware of everything around you.

#11. We all get hung up on what others think of us, both good and bad. The bottom line is that what others think of us is none of our business. The only thing that matters is what *you* think of yourself.

# THE UP SIDE OF DOWN

Let me tell you about a Viennese friend of mine, whose 75th birthday party I attended. This friend responded to well-wishers at his party with a toast: " I want to share with you, my friends, that the first fifty years of my life were horrible; I went through the war, lost my family and fortune, and for many years after that it seemed as if I couldn't do anything right. But the last twenty-five years have been absolutely marvelous!"

Even after fifty years of trouble, heartache, and some misery, my friend was able to turn his fortune around and really learn to enjoy life. He knew that it was never too late to go after your dreams and find happiness, even when life has dealt you a rough hand. His story perfectly illustrates one of the most important things that you have to remember if you want to lead a rich and fulfilling life: that there is an *up* side to every down: there is always a chance to make your life better. I may be a dreamer, and some people have called me naive, but I truly believe that you can make your life better if you are able to understand this important fact.

Every life has balance - the good and the bad, the up and the down, etc. You can't escape this, no matter how much you wish that life was perfect all of the time. But life isn't perfect. The key to enjoying *your* life, though, is to find the good in the bad experiences.

Ask yourself the question, "What do I gain from losing?" Learn how to find the silver lining in your own personal storm clouds. You may not believe this, but illness, disappointment, and loss often have hidden advantages once you learn to look deeply at these negative experiences. There are lessons in success, but failures can teach you much, much more.

I am here to show you that you can find strength in failure, that you really can turn around all those bad things that have happened to you. You just have to learn to see the down times in your life as an opportunity for growth and change, and learn how to extract the good from these difficult times.

Does this sound crazy? Just think about it for a minute. Look at all the good that happens after a natural disaster. In times of tragedy, such as 9/11, people come together to offer money, time, and support. Heroes come out of the woodwork. The human spirit triumphs over this adversity. And look at what good has come out of the suffering of some of humanity's greatest people, such as Jesus, Gandhi, and Martin Luther King, Jr. Jesus was put to death. Gandhi and King did jail time in their efforts to bring about a better life for others, and then were killed for their beliefs. But imagine life without the fruits of their labor and suffering.

These people changed the world as we know it. They were put on earth to make a difference, but it wasn't an easy thing to do. Though your aspirations may be more humble, there is something wonderful to learn in these examples. To fulfill your own destiny, whether it is to be the best mother or father you can be, a successful lawyer, a nurse, a politician or whatever, you will only be able to do good for yourself and others if you bounce back from your down times and persevere through your troubles. You bring power to the next generation.

I am here to help give you the strength to look at life in a whole new way, to approach your experiences with a more positive, life-affirming attitude, and to break out of the negative down cycle you may be in. You are not alone if you feel that it is impossible to see the good in life. Many weeks I receive many thousands of letters, mostly from people who have written to me to say that they were stuck in down cycles in their lives and needed help getting out. What they wanted from me was hope - hope that tomorrow would be a better day and that I could rid them of whatever "curse" was plaguing their lives.

From my years of experience, though, I can tell you that there is no "curse," that bad things will always happen to good people no matter what. And I can't guarantee you that tomorrow will necessarily be a better day. But I *can* tell you that a better day will come. I've seen it happen a million times. I've only helped these people, like I will help you, get through those difficult days, the ones that come to all of us sooner or later, the days when we almost wish we could just die and get life over with.

After hundreds of thousands of letters from people needing help and hope, I began to see the value in these down cycles. They are important for a few reasons. You appreciate the good times so much more when you've suffered the bad.

But there are other benefits, other things to learn when you go through a down time, a real way to understand the up side in every down. Let me give you a few examples so that you can understand what I am talking about.

I know of a big-time company president who has his own way of handling problems. Every time he runs into a problem, he writes it down on a piece of paper and puts it in a box on his desk. Then he forgets about it. Every Wednesday, after lunch, he tips out all the pieces of paper from his problem box onto a table. He reads through each one. Many of the "problems" have already been taken care of, and he throws them away. The ones that haven't go back into the box until next week.

The point here is that many problems take care of themselves. This company president has found a way of successfully dealing with the things at work that could get him down. It's all in your attitude, the perspective you take. If you look at these difficulties as something that can conquer you, they will. But if you put them in a box and let time, God, and your subconscious work on them, *you* will conquer these problems.

Every successful person whom I have met has overcome bad times. These people realize that the down side of life occurs to make you see more clearly. Interestingly, one's true qualities come to the surface during these down times: courage, hidden abilities, sense of humor, and so on. I know that most of my best learning experiences have come about when I was going through a hard time.

Some time back, when I was going through a rough patch in my life, I joined a club that met each week. I asked to be the "warm-up" man for famous international guest speakers, to put the audience in a good mood. At that time in my life, that was the last thing on my mind. I was feeling very down and sorry for myself, and nothing seemed funny to me. But I decided to make an effort at being a good warm-up man, and I even bought books filled with jokes.

My first effort at being a stand-up comic was a disaster. So was the second. And - ouch - the third. My audience, many of whom were senior citizens, just sat there frowning at me. What could I do to make them laugh? A well-meaning friend advised me to quit, but I vowed to persevere. I watched comedians on TV, I asked guests at dinner parties to tell me jokes, I did everything I could to learn how to get over this obstacle and establish rapport with the audience. And sure enough, it happened! I actually got these people to laugh, and it felt wonderful. Laughter is infectious.

Now I laugh too, with them, at myself, at anything. My life picked up when I took on the attitude that I could learn something from this down time in my life. And I did.

I hope you see that there are lessons that you can only learn during temporary failure and defeat. It is important to see this as only *temporary*, though, a momentary down cycle. That's why you must never take no for an answer. Maybe all you need to do is rethink, regroup, change your direction. If John Logie Beard had given up, there would have been no television. If

Alexander Graham Bell had given up, no telephone. Bill Gates quit Harvard, but he stuck with the idea of Microsoft. These people achieved something because of hard work, persistence, and some luck. They learned something in their failures and used this knowledge to create success.

So say "Thank you Lord" when these learning opportunities come up. When a door slams in your face, say to yourself, "If I have to bang on that door a hundred times before it opens, I will." And knock on that door again - harder and better - until it opens.

Most people during their down times are really planting seeds and doing all they can in preparation for when the pendulum of life takes an up swing. So open your eyes, especially in times of trouble, and never give up. There's always an up side to being down.

Isn't life *great*?

To make life greater, repeat this program from time to time.

To order more Humanics books
please visit our website at

# www.humanicspub.com

# VISIT deartony.com

ISBN 978-0-89334-889-2
90000

PRINTED IN THE UNITED STATES

9 780893 348892

CPSIA information can be obtained at www.ICGtesting.com
Printed in the USA
BVOW030603041111

275140BV00003B/7/P